HISTORY MAKERS

THE ROMANS

Clare Oliver

p

CONTENTS

This is a Parragon Book
This edition published in 2003

Parragon
Queen Street House
4 Queen Street
Bath BA1 1HE, UK

Copyright © Parragon 2002

Produced by

David West ☗ Children's Books
7 Princeton Court
55 Felsham Road
Putney
London SW15 1AZ

British Library Cataloguing-in-Publication Data

A catalogue record for this book is available from the British Library.

ISBN 1-40540-964-9

Printed in Dubai

Designers
Julie Joubinaux, Rob Shone

Illustrator
Mike Lacey (SGA)

Cartoonist
Peter Wilks (SGA)

Editor
James Pickering

A MIGHTY EMPIRE
4

RULING ROME
6

ON THE MARCH
8

BUILT TO LAST
10

TRADING PLACES
12

FOLLOWERS OF FASHION

14

HOME, SWEET HOME

16

IN THE FAMILY

18

LATIN LEARNING

20

FEELING PECKISH?

22

AT THE BATHS

24

THAT'S ENTERTAINMENT!

26

GODS & GODDESSES

28

A MESSY END

30

INDEX

32

A MIGHTY EMPIRE

NEARLY 3,000 YEARS AGO, people began farming around the place we call Rome, in Italy. Over time, their farms became villages and their villages grew into towns.

Eventually, Rome was a big, bustling city that controlled a mighty empire. Lands the Romans had conquered stretched for thousands of kilometres, across Europe, Asia and Africa.

YOU MUST BE JOKING!
The Romans set up their own postal service called the *cursus publicus*. Horseback messengers galloped around night and day, delivering important documents to all corners of the enormous empire. It must have been exhausting work!

OFF MY LAND!
To gain new lands, the Romans had to defeat the peoples already living there. Over 70,000 Romans died in southern Britain when the fierce queen Boudicca decided to fight back!

CAN YOU BELIEVE IT?
Rome had a birthday.

YES. The Romans believed that their city was 'born' on 21 April 753 BC. They said it was founded by twin brothers called Romulus and Remus. The city marked the spot where a she-wolf had rescued the twins when they were babies.

Seven hills of Rome
Rome was built on and around seven hills. The hills made a natural defence but once Rome was rich and powerful, it was protected by thick city walls, too.

RULING ROME

IN THE EARLY DAYS, KINGS RULED ROME. The last king was Tarquin the Proud – but he wasn't so proud after the people overthrew him!

For the next 400 years or so, Rome was a republic. Each year, the Romans voted for two consuls who shared the job of governing. Finally, in 27 BC, a man called Augustus seized power. He was the first of Rome's emperors.

YOU MUST BE JOKING!
Many emperors were good and ruled wisely, but not all. Emperor Nero was barking mad! He's said to have set fire to Rome and cackled away as the city burnt to the ground.

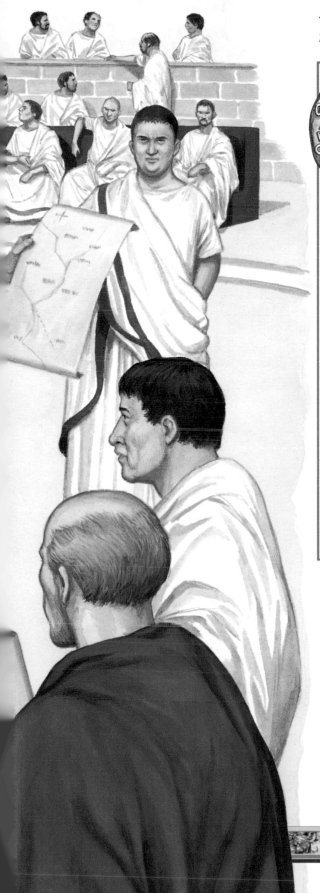

The emperor and his senators

The Roman emperor had a group of around 300 noblemen who advised him and helped him to rule. They were called the Senate.

A DOG'S LIFE

Slaves did all the hard work in ancient Rome. To show who they belonged to, slaves had to wear a metal disc, rather like a dog tag. Slaves were bought and sold at market, just like animals. Some lucky slaves were freed, though, as a reward for good service.

CAN YOU BELIEVE IT?
All the senators were men.

NO. Most were, but according to some stories there was one very strange exception. Emperor Caligula was so loony that he made his horse a member of the Senate!

YOU MUST BE JOKING!
Wounded soldiers wore spiders' webs! The sticky silk helped the skin to knit together. Tucking a bundle of herbs into the bandage was another trick – it killed any germs.

ROME'S 300,000-STRONG ARMY was split into legions of 5,000 soldiers. These were posted all over the empire to capture new lands, guard them, and to control local rebels. The men travelled huge distances, usually on foot.

Shell of shields
Roman soldiers advanced in a tortoise shape. Their shields acted as a shell, protecting them from attack.

Roman soldiers had to buy their own armour and weapons, which included javelins, swords and daggers. They were builders as well as fighters. Their roads linked all the parts of the empire, and their forts and walls defended its borders.

ATTACK OF THE ELEPHANTS!

In the third century BC, Rome fell out with Carthage, an important North African port. Carthage's general, Hannibal, led a vast army all the way to Italy. His war elephants terrified the Romans, but Hannibal was forced back in the end.

BUILT TO LAST

The Romans invented central heating.

YES. Rich people's homes had heating. The warmth came from an underfloor wood-burning fire, looked after by slaves. There were gaps under all the floors so the warm air could flow.

THE ROMANS were brilliant builders and engineers. They learnt how to make clay bricks last longer by firing them in hot ovens, and they invented measuring instruments that architects still use. They also discovered how to build arches and huge, domed roofs.

Many Roman buildings and roads still stand. The Romans laid more than 85,000 km of super-straight roads to tie together their empire.

Laying a road
Roads were built from layers of sand, stones, gravel and, finally, paving slabs. They curved, so any rain drained away.

YOU MUST BE JOKING!
The Romans made the first cement by mixing volcanic ash, lime and water. Like modern cement it had to be used quickly – before it set!

WONDER WATERWAYS
The Romans built bridges called aqueducts to carry drinking water into their cities. To take the weight of all the water flowing along them, aqueducts were supported on rows of strong arches.

TRADING PLACES

THE BUSY PORT OF OSTIA lay about 10 km from the city of Rome. Each day, merchant ships arrived from all over the empire – and beyond – loaded to the gunnels. They brought grain, timber, wool, silk, spices and slaves.

Not all goods had to be shipped in. Grapes, olive oil and other products from Roman farms came into the city by road on simple carts.

At the harbour Ostia was built on the Mediterranean coast, at the mouth of the river Tiber. Merchants' goods – and catches by Ostia's fishing fleet – were taken upriver to Rome by barge.

YOU MUST BE JOKING! Traders sometimes fiddled their weights. Port and market officials had the job of checking weights and measures to make sure customers weren't being swindled.

THE ROMAN SHOPPING CENTRE

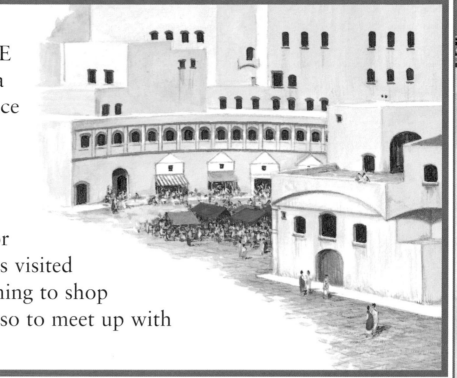

Trajan's Forum was a five-storey marketplace in the centre of Rome. It had business offices, as well as 150 shops and an open space for market stalls. Citizens visited the Forum each morning to shop and to haggle, and also to meet up with family and friends.

CAN YOU BELIEVE IT?
The Romans used banknotes as well as coins.

NO. They had no paper money. Roman coins were cast in bronze or silver. Early coins didn't even have fixed values.

THE ROMANS wore simple tunics woven from wool or – if they were rich – from linen, cotton or silk. Over this, women wore a dress called a *stola*, and men wore a cloak, or *toga*. This was held in place with a handsome brooch.

Getting ready
Slave girls helped to dress their mistress, style her hair and apply her make-up.

ALL THAT GLITTERS

Ordinary people wore bronze and glass jewellery, but the rich really showed off their wealth. Their golden necklaces, bracelets, rings and brooches were set with costly gems. Both men and women used perfume and make-up. Cosmetics were stored in pretty jars or pots.

But not every man in the empire wore a toga. Celts ruled by the Romans wore warm, checked trousers, while in Egypt, the men wore cool linen kilts.

CAN YOU BELIEVE IT?
Roman footwear had hobnails.

YES. Travellers and soldiers needed sturdy footwear to survive miles of marching. Their leather soles were studded with nails to stop them wearing out.

YOU MUST BE JOKING!
Most Roman ladies were naturally dark-haired, but being fair was the height of fashion. Some bought blonde wigs made from the hair of Germanic slaves, but others bleached their own. The dye was a mix of lye (urine and ash) and vinegar. It must have smelt terrible!

HOME, SWEET HOME

WEALTHY ROMANS lived in spacious, one-storey homes. The hall, or atrium, was more like a courtyard than a room, with an opening in the ceiling to let in light. This was where the family entertained guests.

CAN YOU BELIEVE IT?
Roman guard dogs were made of glass and stone.

YES. Mosaics of guard dogs warned burglars to steer clear. The pictures sometimes came with the words *cave canem*: 'Beware of the dog!'

THE HIGH LIFE
In the largest cities, many people lived above the shops in blocks of flats. Some flats were small and poky, but not all. A few had as many as a dozen rooms.

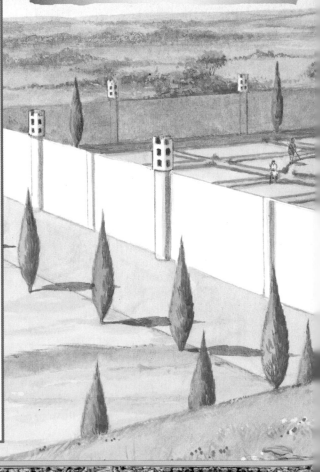

Doors off the atrium opened into the family rooms, kitchens, garden and slave quarters. Homes like this were found in town and country – but only noble families could afford to live in them. Most ordinary people lived in shacks or flats.

Country life
Wealthy Romans might own a huge country house, or villa rustica, with large gardens and lots of farmland.

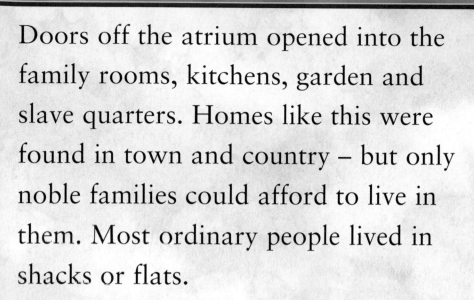

YOU MUST BE JOKING!
The Romans kept snakes – not real ones, but pictures of them. They thought that snakes brought good luck. People also had household shrines, where they made offerings each day to the gods.

IN THE FAMILY

A ROMAN FAMILY meant everyone who lived in the same household. As well as a husband, his wife and their children, it included any slaves that they owned. Everyone in the household had to answer to the father, or *paterfamilias*.

Housework
Home life was never quiet. Rich families had lots of children – and lots of busy slaves!

CAN YOU BELIEVE IT?
Romans wore wedding rings.

YES. And Roman brides wore veils and carried flowers, too. The bride and groom signed a contract to become man and wife, just as people do today.

The mother gave orders to the slaves and organised the day-to-day running of the house. She also helped her husband choose who their children would marry.

CHILDHOOD TOYS
Roman children had marbles, spinning tops, dolls and model animals to play with. But poor children had little time for toys – they had to work or help their parents.

YOU MUST BE JOKING!
Many Roman families kept dogs, cats or ornamental fish as pets. Doves were another favourite – and so were tame deer!

LATIN LEARNING

YOU MUST BE JOKING!
Teachers were mostly clever Greek slaves – not native Latin speakers at all! There were few schools, so some children from rich families had live-in tutors.

Off to school
School boys studied reading, maths and public speaking. Their sisters usually stayed at home to learn how to run a household instead.

THE LANGUAGE of the Romans was Latin, named after the first people who lived around Rome, the *Latini*. Latin had most of the same letters as our alphabet but no little letters, only capitals.

Latin was carved on milestones and monuments, and stamped on coins. It was used for writing important records on papyrus scrolls or books of vellum (calfskin).

Latin was the official language. Locals learnt it to talk to their Roman rulers, but they kept alive their own languages, too.

CAN YOU BELIEVE IT?
Roman school boys wrote in exercise books.

NO. They practised their writing on wax tablets, using a pointed stylus. They could melt the wax to reuse the tablet again and again!

LETTERS COUNTED
The Romans used mixtures of letters to stand for different numbers. Seven was VII (a five and two ones). To count like this, Romans had to be able to add up – no wonder they used abacuses!

I - 1
V - 5
X - 10
L - 50
C - 100
D - 500
M - 1000

FEELING PECKISH?

ROMANS STARTED the day with a simple breakfast of bread with olives or fruit. For lunch, there was more bread, served with vegetables and cold meat, fish or cheese.

The main meal began around four o'clock. Most Romans did not have a kitchen, so they bought hearty soups and stews from a local tavern. Richer Romans feasted on roast meats, fish and shellfish, eggs, flans and vegetables, with fresh fruit for dessert.

YOU MUST BE JOKING! Honey-roast dormouse was a delicacy in ancient Rome! Cooks kept the mice in terracotta jars and fattened them up for a few weeks first. That made them extra meaty!

Tucking in
Romans did not sit up to eat their main meal. They reclined on long couches and ate off low tables. Feast foods were lavish. Roast pig was a favourite – and so was quail, ostrich or swan!

CAN YOU BELIEVE IT?
The Romans used to throw up at dinner parties.

YES. At a banquet, slaves served up course after course. Sometimes people made themselves sick just so that they could fit in more food!

IN THE KITCHEN
The Romans liked their food spicy. For one thing, strong flavours helped to disguise rotten meat. A widely-used sauce was *liquamen* – fish and salt pounded up with a mortar and pestle.

23

AT THE BATHS

Every major Roman town and city had at least one public baths. There were special times for men and women to bathe. People went to the baths to get clean, but also to relax and meet up with their friends.

Romans liked to play dice or read while they were at the baths. If they were feeling energetic, they might lift weights or play ball games.

YOU MUST BE JOKING!
Romans went to the toilet together! People could chat together in public loos because there were several seats side by side. There was no toilet paper – people wiped their bottoms with a sponge on a stick.

Bathing, Roman-style

First stop was a dip in a cool-water pool. Then bathers relaxed in the tepid pool before getting into a hot, steamy pool. Next, the skin was scraped clean in a hot, dry room. Finally, there was a refreshing plunge in an icy-cold pool.

CAN YOU BELIEVE IT?
The Romans worked up a soapy lather.

NO. The Romans didn't use soap. To get clean, they rubbed olive oil into their skin, then scraped it away with a metal strigil. Dirt and dead skin came away with the oil.

BATH SLAVES
The baths employed lots of slaves. Some worked underground, looking after the furnace. The rest kept the place clean and looked after customers. They plucked hair, scooped out ear wax, gave massages, brought fresh towels and served drinks and snacks.

THAT'S ENTERTAINMENT!

The Romans' favourite entertainment was a trip to watch the gladiators. These were prisoners or slaves who had been trained to fight. They fought to the death, either against each other or fierce wild beasts such as bears, lions or tigers.

In Rome, the best fights took place in a 50,000-seat amphitheatre called the Colosseum. The floor of the arena was covered in sand to soak up all the blood.

Mortal combat
Some gladiators were equipped with only a fishing net and a long fork called a trident. Others wore armour and carried swords or daggers.

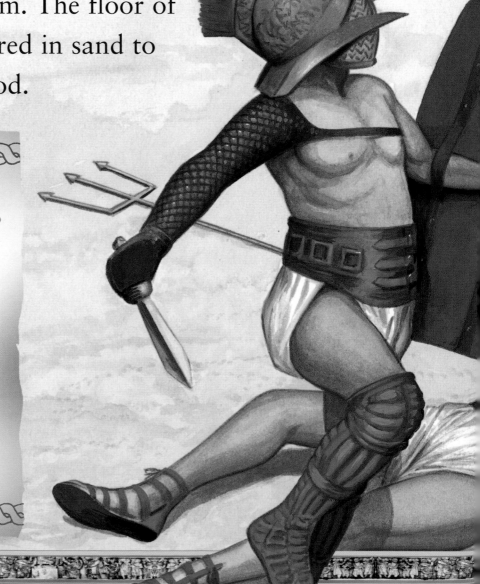

CAN YOU BELIEVE IT?
The Colosseum was flooded on purpose!

YES. But not for swimming galas! It was so spectators could enjoy pretend sea battles, with the gladiators fighting from real boats.

CIRCUS MAXIMUS

Chariot-racing was another top spectator sport. Horse-drawn chariots galloped around oval racetracks called *circuses*. Rome's Circus Maximus had room for 250,000 spectators and sometimes put on as many as 24 races a day.

YOU MUST BE JOKING!

The Romans had pantomimes! A *pantomimus* was an actor who told a story to music. He didn't speak, though – the audience guessed the story from his gestures and from the different masks that he wore.

OH YES HE DID!

GODS & GODDESSES

THE ROMANS prayed to hundreds of different gods. Even the emperor made sacrifices to the gods to keep them happy.

Each god looked after one aspect of people's lives. Vesta was goddess of the hearth. Priestesses kept alight a holy flame so that she would look after the Romans' homes.

King of the gods
Jupiter was the most important god. He ruled over all the others – even Juno, his wife!

YOU MUST BE JOKING!
Like most Romans, the Emperor Augustus was extremely superstitious. He always put on his right shoe first, because he believed that left was unlucky. Strangely, the Latin word for 'left' was *sinister*!

Other gods important in the home were the family spirits (*lares*) and store-cupboard spirits (*penates*). There was even a goddess of door hinges!

1 *Jupiter, king of the gods*
2 *Mars, god of war*
3 *Apollo, god of healing*
4 *Neptune, the sea god*
5 *Juno, queen of the gods*
6 *Venus, goddess of love*
7 *Diana, goddess of the Moon and hunting*

CAN YOU BELIEVE IT?
Romans cursed in temples.

YES. If a Roman didn't like someone, he wrote their name and a curse on a bit of pottery. He left the curse at a temple, so the gods would make it come true.

A FOREIGN GOD
Mithras was the Persian god of light and war. After Persia became part of the empire many Romans, especially soldiers, began to worship Mithras. They sacrificed bulls at temples built in his honour.

A MESSY END

EVENTUALLY, the Roman empire was so big that it was impossible to rule – or to defend. The Emperor Diocletian split the empire in two in AD 293, but the western half just grew weaker and weaker.

Rome in flames
Visigoths overran Rome in AD 410 and the city was invaded again in 455 by the Vandals. The western empire finally fell in 476 and the emperor toppled from power.

CAN YOU BELIEVE IT?
We remember the Romans all year round.

YES. They invented most of our calendar. January is named after Janus, their two-headed god of new beginnings.

Barbarians raided the borders. Slowly, western lands were lost to Picts, Saxons, Visigoths, Vandals, Huns and other fearsome peoples.

YOU MUST BE JOKING!
Pompeii escaped the barbarians, because it had been buried in ash from a volcano in AD 79! Finds from the town have told us loads about everyday life, including what the Romans ate.

EAST AND WEST
Although the western empire fell in the AD 470s, the eastern part survived for another thousand years. It's known as the Byzantine Empire, because its capital was Byzantium.